Table of Contents

This book is dedicated to those who lost their minds in love. The ones who wanted more than he or she was given. There is life after letting go. You have to want to go through the process of healing first though. You deserve love. You don't deserve toxicity. Time and recovery heal all wounds. I know what it's like to detox from bad emotional and mental bonds with a person. You can do this.

Delusional

When I Lost My Ever-Loving Mind

DELUSIONAL
/dəˈlo͞oZH(ə)nəl/

adjective

characterized by or holding false beliefs or judgments about external reality that are held despite incontrovertible evidence to the contrary, typically as a symptom of a mental condition

By Candi Usher

Introduction

I was delusional. I thought he loved me. I felt I could change him. But he didn't love me like he claimed he did. His mouth said one thing, his actions another. I intentionally blinded myself to what he was doing. I ignored his actions, thinking my love could do enough to make him want to be different. One thing about a man who is allowed to keep doing wrong is that he will never change. I was delusional in ignoring myself to my almost detriment and demise. Oh, but the discoveries I made. Want to hear about them? Join me on this journey of former delusions, and the healing and freedom from saying no more.

To be clear, this book does not go from the first of the year to the end of the year. It goes from June 14, our wedding date, to June 14 of the next year. Thought you may need a little context so you don't get confused.

***This is a true account of events. Certain events were left out due to privacy and protection. The same goes for names.**

***If you want to tie the entire story together, you can read "I'm Still Standing Here" and "My Forever Angel"**

Year 2

So...to find the story of how we met, you must read my book "My Forever Angel". I'm not going to relive that part, because technically that was Year 1. Year 2 will deal with what happened after that. Year 2 started on June 14, 2009. I was getting ready to get out of the military. My time was almost up. I had gotten in trouble for "lying" about finding some stupid special paper so an award could be printed (I looked for the paper, asked who I was supposed to ask, and I did what I was supposed to do). I was called a liar, and all.

I didn't care anymore. One thing about it, I had just gone through something extremely traumatic. Did they care? No. I blame myself for not walking away from him and the Navy. I should have asked for a medical retirement, but I thought I was stronger than that. I was stupid. I went through the whole system and was still called a liar when I explained that I wanted to stay and why. I gave up. This fool said he called and pleaded for me to be able to stay in. Yet I was told no one received a phone call. Strike twenty of however many at that point with him. I had to come up with a plan for when I was out. I was willing to work a job, but I wanted to be a stay-at-home mom. With the way his jobs were, that wouldn't be possible. So I started job hunting. That was an absolute disaster. The only jobs that wanted to hire me were looking for someone to do sales and marketing, and I didn't want to deal with people anymore on that level. I wanted to give up so bad.

Amid it all, I still wanted to have another child. Stupid, I know. I wanted to try again in my marriage. I didn't want it to be a failure in yet another marriage. I put my everything into it. I forgave him for what happened before. I wanted my son to have a family. So we tried again for another child. I'm not going to lie though. I lived in a huge fear. I worried that the same thing that happened to my second son would happen again. At the same time, I was scared to talk to a doctor about it beforehand. I knew how the military would look at me. I didn't want them in my business like that, as they had already failed me once. I would never give them that chance again. My heart wanted another child too. I knew that baby would never replace the one I lost. I was still broken over that.

I finished my time in the military, realizing that we now had to find a place to go. We moved in with his mom for a little while, but that was not the place to be, as we had already lived with her before, and wanted to continue the independence of living on our own. We moved into a hotel until we could find a place. My oldest son was glad to be starting school. I was hoping he would do better because preschool was not the best for him. He had an issue with women being in charge because of abuse that happened when he was younger from what was supposed to be a family member. I was concerned if he would be able to adjust. The military suggested that he have counseling, but their counseling services were awful. They were more concerned about the issues affecting my job, over him getting help. My hope and prayer was that the new school year wasn't going to be as full of issues.

We moved into the hotel right before the school year started. I had received my DD 214 (the paper that said I was released from my duty to the military) and was free. I found out that Veteran Affairs was offering a program called Post 9/11, a program for Veterans to go to school that offered more time than the Montgomery GI Bill. I decided to sign up, and encouraged my husband to sign up too, as he was a Veteran also. I figured it would be great to earn a degree and get paid at the same time. Plus, there was the offer of an advance for starting, which we couldn't pass up. It was enough money to help and put a deposit down for an apartment. What I wasn't expecting was the surprise that came next.

So, I woke up sick for a few days before receiving our advance. I didn't think much of it, as I had been under so much stress, and I had experienced medical issues in the past. I figured it wasn't that serious. My husband told me I was pregnant, and to take a test. I know that had to be a lie. There was no way I was pregnant. Took the test. It was blatantly positive. I was in shock, but I was excited and scared too. Not knowing what happened medically to my son. Also, knowing what my husband had done the first time. There was a part of me that just wouldn't trust him anymore. I should have listened to it. Some time passed, and I had found an obstetrician. Because my husband was not working as much, I figured he could come to the appointments with me and be more involved. That didn't happen. I had my pregnancy confirmed and my first appointment by myself. I returned home, and he headed to work after we argued. His laptop was open. I looked at it, and it was unlocked. His MySpace was open, and lo and behold, he was messaging the same ex that was a problem the first time. I confronted him, and he claimed he let a friend get on his laptop, and that it was him that contacted her from his (my husband's) page. I tucked the info away. I knew in my heart he was lying.

School for us eventually started, and it was a rocky start. We were still living in a hotel, and applying for an apartment. We also had to make sure my son was getting to school on time. We managed to pull things together though. None of our classes were together, considering that I was going to school for Information Technology and he was going to school for Criminal Justice. He and I made sure we always met for breaks and lunch. I noticed that there was this little Caucasian girl who started to hang around him a lot. She was like a little puppy. Everywhere he went there she was. She had a pronounced disdain for me, which almost got her knocked out a few times. Several friends that I had made had to make me walk away a few times. It was just the first semester of school, and all hell was already breaking loose. I asked him to deal with the issue more than once. I even confronted the young lady and let her know that as his wife, which she knew I was, her actions were disrespectful and that his actions were too. Neither of them seemed to care. His teachers even got on his case about how he was acting. He claimed she was going through some things with an abusive boyfriend and he was just trying to help. One morning, she called at 1 a.m. He took the call and then said he was going to take her somewhere. It took him almost 3 hours to come home. He went straight to bed, with no explanation. I tucked it away in my mind. Yes, I know I gave him too many chances. I loved him way more than he deserved.

We continued the rest of the semester with him still giving her attention. They had a school project, and somehow he became the gangster in the video their group was creating, and she was playing his girlfriend. There was nothing I could do about it, but I was at every taping of the video. I was just tired of it all. I was very pregnant, so my attitude was already off the charts. Once again, she called him in the middle of the night, this time to supposedly take her to the bus station so she could leave town. He took hours to come home, then wanted to touch me when he arrived back. Ummm....no sir. You didn't even take the time to wash the stench of her off of you. I'm not going to lie. I was glad she was gone. And no, that didn't excuse to absolve him of his issues. I wanted to keep pressing forward though since our son would be arriving soon.

Being pregnant had me always hungry. We would stop at Hardee's by the school for breakfast. We always ate biscuits and gravy with coffee. Decaf coffee for me. I couldn't do the orange juice because it makes me itch. After school, we would find a restaurant to go eat at. My friend would most of the time ride with us, then we would bring her back in time for her to catch her bus, or just take her home.

Year 3

We were now in the third semester of school. My oldest had been doing well in school, having finally settled into school. My husband and I had just celebrated our 3rd anniversary. The arrival of my third son was quickly approaching. I had to take all my final exams early because I didn't want to have to take the tests with a fresh c-section cut. My doctor kept a close eye on me since the last pregnancy had ended so badly. I was constantly being monitored and chewed out for the times my blood pressure was too high. Granted, all the drama didn't help. The day finally came for my appointment on Monday, June 14, the day after our anniversary. I was told if I had dilated to 3 cm, I could have my c-section. I was checked, and the doctor said we could head over to the hospital, which was right down the street. I couldn't contain my excitement. I was so ready to see my son's face. We had made it this far in the pregnancy with no complications. I just wanted to hear him cry. Everything happened quickly, and my son entered the world with the greatest cry I had heard since my oldest was born. My husband went over and cut the cord, and held his son. At that moment, I made up my mind to just try to keep moving forward for my kids. Yes, I was stupid. Yes, I still wanted to believe in him.

He named our second son after himself again. He was the doting father, at least at that point. He stopped picking up his other son though. It was like there was an intentional disconnect. I wanted him to bring him around because no matter what, the boys were brothers and should have spent time around each other. He decided he didn't want to, and I left it there. My friend came to spend time with me at the hospital so I could rest. My son looked at her and started yelling at her on purpose. It was so funny to me. My stomach and stitches hurt so bad from my laughing. She handed him to me, and he stopped yelling. I knew right then that the two of them were going to get along great.

I spent 2 weeks away from school, then I went back. It was a little hard going back because I didn't want to be away from my baby. The blessing was that the girl across the street was looking for a job, so we hired her as our babysitter. Things seemed to be going smoothly. My grades were on point. But things still seemed off for some reason. One day, we were sitting in the house, when it seemed like the walls were moving. I realized it was an earthquake, and immediately ran to get my sons from upstairs. As soon as I brought them down, the apartment shook again. It wasn't strong, but it was enough to have you praying it wouldn't get stronger. I was ready to move at that point. Later on that month, my oldest son turned 7. I had a party at my friend's sister's house. My husband wouldn't even come. Things between us felt different.

That year we also got sick for the first time. The flu had been going around the school. My house got slammed by what felt like a ton of bricks. It started with my son being sick. Then my husband got sick. I was the last one and was hit the hardest. Fortunately, we were between semesters, so we didn't lose any time. I was a hot mess. I felt like someone had beat me with a bat. I hadn't been sick like that in a long time. It hadn't been that bad since my pregnancy with my second son when I was sick all day every day. We still had to get up and take the oldest to school and pick him up because where we lived was too close to the school, so no bus ran nearby.

Oh, did I mention that my husband's second son's brother went to the same school as my oldest? Yep. And they were in the same class. All heck broke loose from that. The boy decided it was a good idea to tell my son, who didn't know his stepfather had another son, that his stepfather was his brother's dad. Blows were thrown. I got to meet the second son's mother face-to-face. My husband kept telling me to stay away from her. I wasn't trying to go near her. I was no threat. What wasn't going to happen was her son was not going to bully my son. There were a few times when we would be standing outside waiting for the kids to be released. She would be on her phone, side-eyeing me, making little snide remarks. That let me know that my husband and her were probably having conversations the times I wasn't there. At one point, she was scared that I wanted to fight her. ***If I wanted to lay hands on her I would have.*** Why would I fight you, who was married at the time you slept with my husband, created a child, and then lied to both men about who the daddy was? Nope. She was not worth the energy.

I used to hang out at my best friend's house often. It allowed me to get away for a while with the kids. I needed some time to relax and just have someone to talk to. Her boyfriend would barbecue almost every time I came over. Her daughter and my son were best friends also. She was the daughter I never got to have. She was my baby. This best friend was there with a few others that I was stationed with in California who were there for me when I lost my second son. My sons were their nephews. My husband didn't like me going to her house. He didn't like her for whatever reason. None of my best friends liked him much. But I chose him just like he chose me. They supported me just like I supported them.

My son's first birthday came, and I threw the most fun party. My girls came by with their kids, and my baby had a blast. He had started walking not too long before. He was bribed by his dad with money. That's how he got him to walk. It worked in its way though. My husband once again disappeared during the birthday party. I don't know if it was about the attention or what. My friends talked to me about it, but I didn't listen to what they had to say. We enjoyed the rest of the party, and my girls gave me and my babies the love that we needed at that time.

Year 4

This was the craziest year. This was 2013, my year of graduation. I was so excited. I was finally at the end of my tumultuous journey in school. I had pushed through pregnancy, moving, drama, and health issues. I couldn't wait!! The thing is, when my day of graduation came, September 13, certain people tried to make it miserable for me. The plan going into the last semester of school was that he would still go to my graduation, even though he didn't get to finish. Again, he quit when the last semester came around, even though he could have pushed through to finish. He decided he wanted to work full-time. He had my whole backing to receive help with anything he needed help with from me, especially child support. He still chose to do it his way, and I supported him in that too. Yet, you want to damper my day. This man decided on the day of my graduation he wasn't going to go. He didn't want to bring the kids either, even though I wanted them all to come. So me and my friend ended up cheering each other on. I cried beforehand though. My heart was so broken. My classmates were amazing. My friend's family couldn't be there for her (they had a legitimate reason), so our classmates cheered for both of us. I won't lie and say I wasn't jealous of those who had their families there. This man did show up to take me out to eat afterward. It felt ingenuine though. He was trying to please me, but it was like his heart wasn't really in it. This was yet another clue to me that he loved me, but I was the only one who was in love. Never him. It felt so lonely there.

I strolled into the new semester. Yep, I signed up for my Bachelor's in Network Management. I wanted to keep learning about what I loved. In the process, he decided that he wanted to move again. This time though, he wanted to move to North Carolina. I was ok with that, as it would put me closer to my family, and the apartment we were looking at was much cheaper than the one we were in. We put in the application, got approved, and started working towards moving. I signed up to go to ECPI so I could continue my bachelor's. Their program was a lot shorter considering I already had credits, and my military experience counted for a lot. In the process of all of that, I found out I was pregnant again.

I had to make this a separate paragraph because it's funny and strange at the same time. So how I found out I was pregnant is I went to the store. On the way to the store, I called my dad. He and I ended up on the phone for almost 2 hours. Yes, when I talk to my dad, I talk to my dad. We have the longest and deepest conversations. When I finally walked into the store, while still on the phone, my husband called. He asked what was taking me so long and if everything was ok. I told him I was on the phone with my dad, and that everything was good. This man randomly says "Oh, and while you're in the store, pick up a pregnancy test." Like what??? There's no way this could be possible. I got off the phone with my dad, grabbed what I needed to, and made a mad dash back to the house. Granted, the store was only five minutes up the road, but it seemed like the longest five minutes in the world. It took forever for the light to change. Everyone and their mama was on the road. I just want to go home and prove this man wrong. I got home, and this man was not wrong. That test popped positive so fast that it wasn't funny. I mean the lines were dark pink. I was happy and mad at the same time. No, we hadn't been careful, but we weren't trying either. I was like, wow. Just wow. That changed so many things for me.

During that process, I received a message from his first son's mother. She said that he was trash and that he was going to treat me the same way he did her. Cheating and all. I didn't want to believe that because I believed him when he said that he wasn't going to take me through the drama again and that he was done talking to other women. Now that I look back, I believe he was trying to talk to her again, and not just about their son. I told him about what happened, and he said that she was just jealous and causing drama. I never understood why he never wanted me to be cool with either of his sons' mothers. Yes, he had two sons before he met me. Yes, I thought I was the one because he married me. Yes, there was consistently egg on my face. Yes, I was desperate to be loved. I wanted to be in love and loved so badly that I accepted any kind of love instead of being patient for true love. I am accountable for my actions. She was trying to warn me, but I didn't listen.

I said goodbye to my classmates. We had had almost 3 amazing years together. I didn't want to leave them because it meant starting over again in a new place. I had become sort of introverted dealing with my husband because he never wanted to go out and didn't like anyone I hung out with. Well, around me he acted like he didn't like them. I'll tell you why later. We moved to a city named Carborro, NC. It wasn't enormous. It was where UNC was though. I was being seen at their hospital for my pregnancy. I also started seeing a therapist. I realized that I had not dealt completely with the death of my son and that my marriage was struggling. I also needed to deal with my first marriage and the pain and trauma that came from that. Sometimes, you realize that you have baggage, and no matter who you're with, your healing is important for you to become the person you want to be. I also needed to do it for my sons. My son deserved a better version of me. I needed to deal with what I felt from my son that I lost. I didn't want to live in fear anymore.

Year 5

I signed up for ECPI to complete their Bachelor's program in Computer Technology. Things were going well. I had a huge problem with the apartment though. We had people of different nationalities living around us, and there were roaches out of this world. Literally. I hated it. And there wasn't much we could do about it. Having 2 kids in that type of environment was ridiculous. My husband found a job at Wendy's at first. If it wasn't for me going to school, we wouldn't have floated the apartment. He finally got a job at Walmart, but it still didn't help with things. Child support ate up most of his money. Because my money only kept the apartment working, I fell behind on my car payments. One night, my husband asked me to come to his job because his car was acting up. I got my sons ready and waddled my way out to where my car was supposed to be. It wasn't there. You could see the drag marks on the ground where the car had been towed. When I tell you the frustration I felt!! I called my husband back and let him know that I couldn't help him and that he would have to figure it out. He began asking 50 million questions. I had already told him I was behind on payments. He knew. Yet, it was still all my fault. I was too angry to care. I took the kids back to the house. It was the first time I didn't have any tears.

My husband finally made it home. We took the car to a shop the next day to figure out what was wrong with it. It was so hot outside it was ridiculous. Being pregnant in the summer was not the business. The mechanic let us know that the fuel pump was going bad. My husband had to tap the gas tank (which contained the fuel pump) with a hammer to get the car to crank. I couldn't go to school anymore because the car wasn't reliable. I was able to find a program that would help pay the rent for a while so that my husband could find something to cover the bills until we got things back on track. He wouldn't do it. He kept working at Walmart. One day, it got to the point where the car stopped working altogether. Blessedly, there was a bus system, so I was still able to go to the doctor and therapy like I needed to. My therapist was very concerned about our situation, especially considering that it was almost time for my son to be born. She wanted to make sure that we were going to be ok. I wasn't sure what we were going to be anymore.

One night, my husband and I were lying on our air mattress. No, we didn't even have a bed, which was awful for my back. It was a two-bedroom apartment, so to keep cool, my sons would sleep in our room. My husband and I were talking. The kids had fallen asleep. I began telling my husband how I felt about everything going on. I was encouraging him to go back to Wendy's since it was close and within walking distance. Depending on the shift, he could even take the bus. He didn't want to do it. I became frustrated and told him that was exactly how I felt. It wasn't right that I was trying to make things happen, and it felt like he didn't even care. This man picked up his box cutter and began cutting his arm. Not enough to go deep or cut a vein, but the cuts were visible. This was probably a hint of where our relationship was headed. I had been at that point before. I had tried to commit suicide. So I didn't even take him seriously. I felt like what he was doing was childish. I took the box cutter from him and got rid of it. I walked outside because I didn't want to breathe the same air as him. I couldn't believe that he would hurt himself with the kids present. I was so over it. I had stopped smoking at the time, but I wanted a cigarette so bad at that point.

My husband eventually sold his car to a salvage place to have a little extra money. It wasn't much and didn't last long. A few days later, he received a letter in the mail that he needed to go to court back in Virginia about child support. It seemed like if it wasn't one thing it was another. I look back now and realize that God was giving me every indication that I needed to leave that man alone. I was so hard-headed. I made labor happen so my son could be born before my husband left. I needed him to be with the kids. My youngest came on October 14. I was stuck 24 times before they found a vein for an IV. The OB (not my OB) tried to get me to have a VBAC. No sir!! I was adamant about my tubes being tied. I wanted no more painful periods. Then I had to be stuck 4 times by a student before the anesthesiologist finally took over and gave me my epidural. Not too much later, I heard the cry of my final child. My Tiny. He was 6 lbs 3 oz. I was moved to recovery, and my husband showed up at the hospital a few minutes later. He and my sons had walked to the hospital from the apartment, which took about an hour and a half. My baby's got to meet the golden baby (the baby after the rainbow baby). My husband held his last child from me. It was a great moment. Those few days in the hospital afterward were perfect. I got some good and much-needed rest. The day came to go home, and we were just going to walk there. But the hospital wouldn't let us leave without a ride. So I ended up having to spend my last $10 on a cab to take us home. Blessedly, we had food because we had food stamps. The messed up part? The lights were cut off the next day. Yeah. We had to sit in the cold and dark. I made sure the kids were bundled up well. Because we had no car, to get food we had to walk to the grocery store, which sucked with having had a c-section and pushing a newborn baby. Like most parents, we made it work though.

The day came that my husband needed to leave. He had called the family that he barely spoke to, and they covered the cost for him to ride the Greyhound bus back to Virginia. Everyone cried when he left, well, except the baby. He didn't care. My sons didn't want to see their father leave. We stood with him as he got on the bus to the Greyhound bus station. In that area, the bus was free, so he could take some free buses, and then pay the fare for the one to Raleigh. I took my children back into the apartment and thought about what I needed to do. I could either choose to find a way to get to my husband in Virginia or go to Georgia with my children until my husband and I were back on our feet. I knew I would have help in Georgia. I also knew that I had promised my father that I would never return. I would come visit but never move back there permanently. In my heart, I knew that if I moved back to Georgia I probably wouldn't want to go back to my husband. I talked to my family, and they made arrangements so my children and I could ride the Greyhound to Virginia. The kids decided they didn't want to be separated from their father, and I honored that.

I was able to get in contact with one of my friends, and she said the kids and I could stay with her and her family for a little while until we found a place or got into a shelter. I was so grateful for her. Getting on the bus with 3 children is not for the faint of heart. Especially after just having major surgery, your baby isn't a week old yet, and nobody wants to cooperate. On top of that, you and your children aren't sitting exactly together. The people on the bus were so helpful though. There was a guy who sat next to my sons who kept them occupied. The lady next to me and several other ladies made sure that I got a nap in here and there. There were even people who blessed us and fed us, even though I had some food with us. God looked out for us the entire way. When we arrived in Norfolk, my friend was there waiting for us. The hug from her was everything I needed.

We arrived at her house, and I called my husband to let him know we had arrived. This is when I began to discover how he felt about my friends. Yes, this is my first time telling a lot of this, because regardless of how our situation went, he doesn't deserve to get knocked off...yet. I did hear from him that his court date went well, and the judge gave him time to get a job and catch up on the child support. The next day, he came over to her house so he could see me and the kids, and spend the night. I burst into tears, and he asked me why I was crying. I told him how hard things had been and that I was glad to see him. Whatever tears were there before he left North Carolina had dried up. He complained to me the entire time. He was itchy because of dog hair. He didn't feel comfortable around her husband (a man who was being kind enough to give us food and shelter for free). The house was too noisy. He didn't even spend the night like he was supposed to. He left early. The kids were disappointed and hurt. There was nothing I could do though. I told them we would see their dad soon, as we had to go fill out the paperwork so we could get into a shelter. My husband had supposedly been job hunting, not that anything came of that.

We filled out the paperwork and began calling shelters to see if they had any openings. At first, we were going to do separate shelters, with him taking the oldest to a men's shelter, and me going to a women's shelter with the other two. Thankfully, a family shelter had room to take us in. We arrived there and were given a room that didn't even have enough room for a crib. That meant that the baby had to sleep in his car seat or on the bed with us. The intake we filled out required a job search, even though I couldn't do any of that since I had a 3-week-old baby and had just had a c-section. At the time, I was also on Zoloft for depression, so it wasn't a good idea for me to push beyond what I could do. They had a cleaning schedule and tried to get me to do chores. I let it be known that I was not able, and they gave my husband 2 chores instead of one. Even though I was glad to be in the shelter, I had a feeling things were going to get crazy. And they did.

I'm not going to say what happened in the shelter, as I don't want to violate privacy. Things in there did get crazy though. My husband had started back to hiding his phone again. He did finally get a job at 7-11. I went to social services and made sure everyone had medical coverage and got food stamps, and because my husband didn't make enough and had child support, we received welfare for a little while. I needed to make sure we had everything we needed to move out as soon as possible. February of the next year came around, and we were able to get into transitional housing. Did I mention the fact that my getting welfare allowed for his child support to be halted for a while? Here I was helping him again.

I decided to get a partial hysterectomy because my periods were still extremely painful, despite losing weight and having my tubes tied. My options from the gynecologist were partial hysterectomy or dealing with pain until I reached menopause. Also found out I had cysts on my ovaries. I refused to keep putting myself through the horror monthly. I made the best choice for me. Now that I think about it...I don't think my husband was ever really supportive. The dynamics of certain parts of our lives did change after my laparoscopic surgery.

Year 6

We celebrated our 6th anniversary, with our middle turning 4 the day after. Things were starting to look better. The oldest was in school but was having issues with other kids. He was bullied often. I hated it. Then we had issues with the family who was upstairs in transitional housing. Their daughter decided one day on the bus that she didn't like what my son said and stabbed him in the eye with a pencil. She tried to say he hit her, but what later came out was that one of her little friends encouraged her to stab him for whatever it was he said. She had a scratch from where he grabbed her after she tried to stab him again. The parent had called the police on my child and all. The whole family almost got beat up. The head of the program just told us all to stay away from each other. I was not as saved then as I am now.

We finally moved past the issue. My husband had a young lady from his job meet me. She was picking him up and dropping him off at times. I had a suspicion there was more to it, but I wasn't going to jump to conclusions. I wanted proof first. So I waited for my time out.

October came around, and my Tiny (what I called my youngest) and my oldest had their birthday party. I combined them since their birthdays were only a week and some days apart. Tiny was not feeling his smash cake. My oldest on the other hand loved his day. My friend's husband even took him on his first motorcycle ride. He had so much fun. We had made up with the family from upstairs. Things were looking good, but there were things still nagging in the back of my mind.

The holidays came around, and my Tiny decided on Christmas that he wanted to walk. We were eating Christmas dinner. Tiny had been crawling on the floor. He grabbed the cabinet and stood up as he had been doing for weeks. All of a sudden, he let go and started taking steps. One part of me wanted to scream and shout, but the other part shut me up so I wouldn't scare him. I got my husband's attention so he could see it too. My sons clapped for their brother. I no longer had a baby. All my babies were growing up on me.

We ended up moving into another apartment, as the shelter was closing down the transitional housing. We had very little time to get packed and moved. But we made it happen. My husband and I split the rent, with him paying a larger portion since he received more. It was only for a short time. I had still been doing counseling and had filed for disability with Veteran Affairs. The loss of my second son still affected me. I cried on his birthday and death day. We lived not far from where he was buried. My mental health was still awful. I had come off the Zoloft and had attempted Wellbutrin. I was just patiently waiting for my answer.

During that time, I started having other medical issues. While we were in transitional housing, my back popped walking down the steps (3 of them) into our room. To this day, it's still a mystery to me how that happened. The pain had me in and out of the hospital. It was excruciating. Found out that not only had my L5-S1 disc herniated, but I had arthritis through the lower part of my back. I also had degenerative disc disease. So I was sent to pain management. I had pills and injections. I went to physical therapy. Nothing worked. On top of that, I was having issues with hidradenitis suppurativa. I was diagnosed with fibromyalgia and severe migraines. I was completely stressed out. Add the mental issues, and I was a complete wreck. I was still a mom and a wife. Broken or not, I still had to take care of my home. I was on so many medications I didn't even know how I functioned. But I did.

Year 7

They say year 7 can make you or break you. It almost broke me. I had another birthday. We had another anniversary, and my middle turned another year older. I turned around and ended up having the sweat glands under my left arm removed to help control the HS (hidradenitis suppurativa). It took some time to recover. But I made it through. I had to do a little physical therapy to get my arm back. My friends came and checked on me and helped out as much as possible. My husband worked overnight, so he wasn't much help unless he had days off.

Another school year has started. I had an in-school and at-home counselor for my oldest to help him navigate things. He had been diagnosed with ADHD. He was the kind of kid who needed to be constantly occupied, or those intrusive thoughts would take over. I wanted him placed in gifted classes because I knew he was more than smart enough, and it would keep his constantly going mind stable. The school said no because of behavior, even though the remedy for that was gifted courses. Schools can be so stupid sometimes. It's like the parent doesn't know what their child(ren) needs. So my child was stuck being bullied and bored

October came around, and my dad and mom came to visit. We had so much fun together. I had a birthday party for my oldest and youngest and included my parents since my Mom's birthday was in September, and my Dad's birthday was in October. Their visit and the party were right before my back surgery. I had decided to go that route since it was either that option or staying on meds and injections. I didn't want to be on meds anymore. The injections weren't even working. This gave me a chance to spend time with everyone before I went under the knife. What did my husband do during that time you ask? Stay in the room. Come out and eat and go back in the room. So I left him where he was. I didn't want my surgery delayed.

The next day, October 14, was my youngest son's birthday. My surgery was supposed to be at a time when my husband still had enough time to leave for work since it was in another city. The hospital was running behind that day. But my time finally came. I remember almost making it to 10 before the anesthesia kicked in. I didn't do well with it, so they made sure I had the proper antinausea medication also. I woke up to my husband sitting there before he left. He kissed me and was gone. I went back to sleep, then woke up in severe pain. They had me hooked up to Dilaudid. Here's the problem with that. You can only click the button every 6 hours. It didn't even work on the first dose. One of my friends called, and I answered the phone in tears. I don't know what she said or did, but the next thing I knew, they were bringing in morphine. I felt so much better once it kicked in. So many friends called and checked on me. My son's counselor even came by and gave me a card and some food. No matter what I went through I had people who cared. Another one of my friends was there to help watch the kids while I was in the hospital.

After 2 days and learning how to walk with a walking chair, I was able to go home. My husband came and picked me up. We arrived home, and I was able to hug my babies. My youngest was the first one to greet me. He got angry though that I couldn't pick him up. He was too heavy at the time, and I was stiff and in pain. It was arranged for a nurse to come by and do therapy with me for 6 weeks. Those 6 weeks sucked to the fullest. I got to the point where I was using a cane and could walk some distance. Eventually, no more therapy. I still was on pain meds, though not quite as strong. I put on some weight because I was on gabapentin, which didn't help my pain but made me eat. I was so over it. It seemed the surgery flared the fibromyalgia so much worse. During my last visit to the sports medicine doctor for my back, I was diagnosed with failed back surgery. It ended up not helping, and the disc above the surgery site was starting to bulge.

I still had no trust in my husband, and the reason why was about to come out. One night, he came home early because he had cut his finger at work. I also noticed that he had not touched me as much as before, claiming that he didn't want to hurt me. I was the overtly sexual one, so it didn't make sense to me. My pain and my needs were two different things. I managed to talk him into going to the hospital. Before he left to go, he went to the bathroom. I had a nagging feeling he was hiding something. I opened his phone, and I read the message "Hey baby. I hope you're ok. Let me know if you need me and if your finger gets any worse." I'm me. So I confronted him about it. He says that it's just an older lady who would come to his job and check on him. So she's calling him baby? He lied straight to my face because I texted her back. She said she didn't know he was married. Yes, I know it was a pattern with him. What comes next is going to make me feel dumber than ever before.

I noticed at one point that there was a liquid coming from his penis. I thought it was odd, and wouldn't sleep with him because of it. Once again, I got him to go to the hospital. He wouldn't answer me as to what was wrong. So I decided to see my primary doctor. When I sent the message as to the reason why, because I didn't want my husband to know what I suspected, my doctor saw me the same day. She had me do a swab and sent it for immediate testing. She called me on the phone the very next morning. I had bacterial vaginosis, caused by gonorrhea. Yeah, he burnt me a second time. My doctor had the biggest look of pity in her eyes as she sent in the prescription for the antibiotic. The biggest issue with this I had was I had just had back surgery not too long before. When I confronted him about it, he claimed he didn't know how he got gonorrhea. Here's the problem with that. He also said that one of the girls at work had it and he must have sat on the toilet after her. He thought I was stupid. First off, who just tells you they have an STD? Second, you can't get gonorrhea off a toilet seat!! You have to have sex. I was flabbergasted.

Later that night, my mind is going at 100 miles an hour. I decided I was going to cut my hair. He hated it when I cut it. I didn't care at that point. Forget him (not really what I said at that point but I don't curse anymore so you fill in the blank for yourself!!). I began questioning myself. What was I doing wrong? Was it sex? Was I not doing enough? While I was chopping my hair, I called a friend on the phone. What she said to me next blew my absolute mind. We were talking, and I was telling her what was happening. She asked me if I was listening, and I said yes. She then tells me that he had tried to hit on her when we first got to school. He messaged her on MySpace. When she found out he and I were married, she shut it down. He was offering to pick her up in my car and all. This was absolute lunacy to me. My best friend. I was pregnant with his child at the time and he was trying to talk to someone who became my friend. That means he sat there with us every day, went out to eat with us, stared in her face, and acted like he did nothing. I was livid.

The New Year came around. That January, I finally received my answer about my disability benefits. I was approved!! My husband wanted to move back to North Carolina. We traveled to Greensboro this time. The rent was a good price. Guess who was paying that again? Yep. Dumb old me. As book-smart as I was, I was dumb in love. It wasn't like I didn't have a great example of how a man was supposed to treat a woman in my dad. I just ended up with men who were like my mom. My bio mom. I'll explain later. Here we were, packing up to move again.

The apartment we moved to didn't have any people around our age there. There were a lot of older people. I knew this move could be good for all of us. Maybe, just maybe, this man could be different if he was away from what he was used to. We will see.

Year 8

Here we are at year number 8. Yes, I was struggling with loving myself the way I should have. I'm sure by now, many of you have said how stupid I was, how I should have left, and plenty of other things. It is what it is. This was what was going on with me, and my mindset through all of this. You can't say what you would do if you weren't in this situation, or have never been through it.

Year 8 started ok. We were doing better at home. My husband had gotten a job at Walmart again. Now two of my sons are in school. I made sure I bought all of my boys everything they needed. We went outside often, and I had started doing Friday night family game night with them. I would let them pick from Uno, Monopoly, or Life, and we would spend some hours playing. My husband worked overnight, so he didn't participate. I received an increase in my benefits, going from 70 percent to 100. PTSD is no joke. I was still having dreams about my son, and the whole situation.

What my husband didn't know is I was also having dreams and ugly thoughts about what he had done. I was having very intrusive thoughts. I was also starting to have a new medical issue. Constant UTIs. It made no sense to me. I knew there had to be a reason. I had so many that year that it wasn't funny. I'm surprised my kidneys still function now. One night I was in so much pain I needed to go to the hospital. I went to the neighbor's house where my husband was hanging out. I had been calling him. Why didn't he answer? Because he was at the neighbor's friend's house playing pool. Or so he said. Believe him? Nope!! Was he drunk? Yep.

I had started going to church after time. My next-door neighbor's friend was a pastor. She invited me to church. I took the kids since my husband was adamant about not going. He made it clear he wasn't trying to get into the God thing. I still invited him every time we went. Sometimes it was all the kids, other times it was just me and the youngest. I had started to change some things and my thoughts. My husband was not happy with that. I also started being friends with some of the people who lived in the apartment complex. One guy and his mom lived across from us. I would sit with them on their porch, and we would hang out, talk, and play cards or Uno while the kids played. My husband didn't like that either. He wanted me there when he went to sleep and when he woke up. I couldn't believe it. I eventually stopped going around them and going to church. It was better than dealing with the drama.

I also started going to therapy again. I didn't care about this therapist though. She seemed too off-put like it was more for the money than anything. I went because I needed to go, but I made it clear that I wanted to see another therapist. They wanted to send me to the VA in Salisbury, but that was too far away. Eventually, they had me signed up for virtual therapy, which I liked a lot better. I could do it while my sons were at school and have some sort of peace. I went to the car for my sessions because I didn't want my husband to hear things I had to say. I was so irritated over a lot of our arguments. And I do mean arguments. I would want to talk about things on my mind, and it seemed like he didn't want to hear it. If there was something wrong, I wanted to talk about it, see where we were, and make the necessary changes. I could see that things in my life were starting to change again. His changes were not for the better.

I asked him why he had slowed down touching me again. He wanted me to do all the work in bed. He wanted sex to help him sleep. But he did nothing to make sure I had satisfaction. Again, I was the more hypersexual one. I didn't want sex anywhere else but with him. Despite the cheating and all, I remained faithful to our commitment to each other. His reason? The same as stated before. He didn't want to cause me more hurt than I was already having. I found that to be a load of bull. We got into it so bad I walked out of the house in the cold. He was angry because I asked him if he was cheating on me. I was tired. He and my son chased me down in the car. We rode back to the house, and he packed his stuff to leave. Like an idiot, I begged him to stay. That would be my last time doing that.

One day, we figured out that the secretary in the office was stealing the rent payments. Then we were told that we had been missing rent payments. I was ready to leave again. My oldest was being bullied yet again. People at the apartment complex were either moving or leaving in ambulances. The old neighbor had moved out, and the new neighbor had some bad little boys. Her grandson dared to put his hands on my son and ended up with his socks knocked off. My baby does not have hands. He has bear paws. She was angry about what happened and called herself correcting my son. No ma'am. I'm not that mother. She backed off. We didn't speak for days. We had to purchase a new car because the old one had given out. Guess who was the first one to ask me if she could go look at it? I was ready to move desperately.

During this year, I wrote my first books. I wrote two cookbooks and my book "Bondage". The first cookbook I wrote because I wanted to share what I loved to do. Cooking has always been a passion of mine. I would post pictures on my social media and people would ask me how I created a dish. I figured the cookbook would help people open their eyes more to the fun of cooking. The second cookbook was written along with my oldest son. I taught him how to cook when he was ten. I feel every man should know how to take care of himself. I don't want my children out in the world on their own and all they know how to cook is noodles, rice, and maybe chicken. I want them to have a taste of the world right in their kitchens. My third book was "Bondage" (name later changed to "I'm Still Standing Here"). This was a book from my heart. It was about what I went through in my first marriage, told from the view of a girl named Cherise. These weren't the best books in the world, but they were mine. They were from my soul. I asked my husband to help me promote my book and cookbooks. He wouldn't even help. I felt little to no support from him. I was so proud of what I had done. But my friends and family came through. I'm grateful for their love and support. My husband had let the air out of my heart though.

My husband did the searching this time. All I did was make it clear I was not moving into another apartment. I wanted a house. He found one, and we visited Fayetteville, NC to see it. We applied and were approved. We hurried up and left. It was a 3 bedroom house for rent. I figured it would give us the chance to save up some money, build our credit, and eventually purchase our own home since I could get the VA loan. That's not how things went.

Year 9

My oldest was excited about heading to high school, but disappointed because he was stuck with the new kids he met in middle school. Once again, he was in another school where he was bullied. We were at the point where if a kid touched him, he was permitted to lay hands. I was over these kids who always wanted to pick on another child because of his/her size, intelligence, or the way the person dressed. My son was his own person. He dressed in uniforms, but he had certain shoes that he liked. Plus, his feet were huge and still growing.

I was still having some medical issues. I was adamant about getting into pain management. The pain management wanted to keep me on the same medication as what I took in Virginia. I let it be what it was because I knew it wasn't going to work. I just wanted to prove that it wouldn't. The pain management doctor started me on a shot in the sciatic nerve. He was even trying to talk me into a device being placed in the area. What he didn't realize was that I had done all the research. I was a part of pain groups on Facebook. I asked all the questions about treatments people had attempted and had a consensus of what worked and didn't work. I did my homework. I still wasn't listened to by him. I also noticed that I was having dizzy spells, especially when I stood up. I thought maybe it was from high blood pressure or stress. Those were the basis, but not the main cause of the problem. It was yet another issue that I felt ignored about.

My husband had found yet another job at Walmart. The only problem was the last Walmart had screwed him over. They said he missed days of work, even though he had put in a 2-week notice, and let them know in person that we were moving. At least that is what he told me. You know my trust in him wasn't very high. He decided to start doing Uber and Lyft. While doing that, he started looking for at-home jobs since my health was deteriorating and we didn't know why. I didn't know how things were going to work out. I just knew that something needed to happen because I was back taking care of all the bills since his money mainly went into child support. Now if we needed extra groceries, his money did help with that.

I saw my first good therapist here. She was an Air Force Veteran. She understood a lot going on with me. She found a combination of medicines that could help. I had also received a diagnosis of bipolar I disorder. I was given the diagnosis because, during my first marriage, I would have blackouts when my ex-husband was abusing me. I was also having manic episodes that turned depressive very quickly. It wasn't the cause of my hypersexuality though. She felt that was just a part of who I was since I was only seeking it with my husband. I began to talk to her about everything that was going on. She couldn't believe that I was staying with him through everything that had happened. She fussed me out for letting so many things slide. We deeply discussed what happened during my pregnancy and losing my son. Going through it with her was so helpful because I needed to face my emotions fully. I had never done that. The tears flowed freely. It was the first time in years I had cried tears of release instead of pain and anger. I realized that my husband and I didn't discuss what happened like we needed to. Granted, I held him responsible. That doesn't mean I didn't hold myself responsible for allowing the treatment that happened. But facing the fact that the one choice harmed not just my child's life, but mine also. I was ready to move forward with my life. I wanted to make sure my physical and mental health was under control because I was about to embark on a new and freeing journey.

Years 10-12

I combined all of these years because not a lot happened. My husband found a job working from home. He was still doing Uber and Lyft off and on. We purchased a car for me, which added to the payments I was making for everything else, but the car was needed since my husband was working. At the same time, my health was once again deteriorating. The dizzy spells weren't getting any better. They were separate from severe migraines and body pain. My back constantly felt like someone kept walking all over it. No one could ever tell me what the issues were. It just felt like I was dying, and we didn't know why. I wanted to give up so bad. My children were why I kept kicking and fighting.

My youngest was going through a lot in school. He was being picked on for his height. Tiny is very tiny. He never looked his age. Kids in grades under him would tease him and hit him because they were bigger than him. They seemed to forget he has not one, but two big brothers. One may have been in high school, but the other was just a grade above him. They held my middle back because he couldn't pass reading. I know that he hated reading, especially the books they had to read. My son likes action and mystery. Those were not the stories they were reading. He was very protective of his little brother. My oldest was making his way through high school, just trying to get to graduation. It was still a fight for him because he was still being bullied, even though he was taller and had filled out. So he was always laying hands.

At one point, one of the vice principals threatened to send my son to an alternative school. I went off on him so badly. I had requested that my son be sent to a STEM school, because he was more than capable of doing the work, and it would be a start to the field of engineering that he wanted to go into. Once again, they based things off of his behavior, when we had reported what was going on over and over. At one point, my son lost a whole tooth because a kid slammed him to the ground while they were playing basketball. I wanted him out of that school so bad. Oddly enough, God answered that prayer in a way I couldn't imagine.

Right when school was getting ready to end, the pandemic started. I had already decided that I was going to homeschool my middle and youngest because I didn't want them behind, and they just weren't happy where they were. Of course, my husband tried to argue me down at first. This was the first time I actually dug my heels in and let it be known that I was going to do what God told me to do and what was best for my children. Plus, I didn't want to be exposed to COVID because I had a fragile immune system, and I knew fighting it was going to be a problem. I was going to fight for what my children needed first. The schools were teaching the state tests anyway, which was useless for my children to use in the real world. I wanted them to garner the life skills and knowledge they would need when they left to be on their own. They needed to know how to use and save money, budget, use art, history, science, and math, and have a strong standard for reading and comprehension. Not be taught a test that would likely forget the information after taking it. I wanted to be the one to pour into them and guide them on a one-on-one basis. That's what they needed. I wanted them to be better than the men who helped create them. With or without help.

My husband had gotten a job at a place putting pigs on a truck to go to a plant. It was a distant job, and he was funky when he came home. It was decent pay. The amount of gas used was awful though. Plus he couldn't stand the smell of bacon anymore. I liked bacon, sausage, and all parts of the pig. I would set my alarm so I could wake up in the morning and make him something to eat. I always made sure he had food to eat for lunch if he didn't want to eat out. He hated that job with a passion. He had supposedly got into it with someone at the job for calling him the N-word. I don't know what happened. All I know is he came home way sooner than he was supposed to. It seemed like he didn't know how to deal with conflict. He had lost a job at Target for the same reason. I was wondering if the people actually said it or if he just wanted a reason to leave the jobs.

During this time, our other car had stopped working. My husband was using my car to work. What did he do twice? He crashed my car. The entire time we were together and I would drive his car, I would ensure it was well taken care of. He utterly disrespected my car whenever he could. From trying to give women (who were not Uber or Lyft passengers) rides to running into two different people at two different points. I was livid!! And guess who had to come off the money twice to get it fixed both times? Oh, I made sure he paid me back the money. I was not having that. $500+ each time. Seriously? It seemed like every time I wanted to get ahead there was something else taking me backwards. I still wasn't catching all the hints and clues being thrown at me by God. I was willfully ignorant.

By the end of the summer, he received back some money he had been waiting for. We went to a car lot, and he purchased a purple SUV for himself. I was getting my car back and I was so happy. As you know, he treated his vehicle much better than he did mine. It was like pulling teeth just asking him to put gas in it. I was paying for the gas. All I needed him to do was pump it. I told him he could even take the oldest since he was almost 18. He did pay off the rest of what I owed on my car, which wasn't much. Time was winding down for us.

Year 13

We walked into year 13 knowing that there was a change in the atmosphere. Something inside me changed. I don't know what it was. My middle had his birthday. He and my youngest had learned how to ride bikes and were once again constantly outside. I loved it. We spent a lot of time in the large backyard enjoying the time and air. We even put a basketball hoop in the backyard so the kids could have as much fun as possible.

That August began my oldest son's senior year. He had to spend it in class on the computer because everything was shut down. Not that my son minded at all. Also, I was officially homeschooling the middle and youngest. It took some getting used to on my end and theirs. My middle wanted his dad to do the schoolwork with him, so I let them go at it. My youngest was so happy to be homeschooled. All the kids were excelling, and I was loving it. We were able to have more outside time. We didn't leave the house much except for appointments. I didn't even grocery shop much. I had them delivered.

My husband was working an at-home job because nothing was going on with Uber and Lyft during that time. A lot of people were getting sick. It was devastating to watch. Unfortunately, he lost his cousin because of it. It was devastating to him. Then his mom got sick. We believe she had a stroke. I couldn't go with him because of the restrictions. I knew he needed to go though. Hopefully, this would also be a time for him and his brothers to get things together. They had a lot of bad blood from the past that they needed to rectify.

I went home to see my family that February because my brother was in town visiting. I hadn't seen him in years, so I wanted to spend time with him. I was avoiding a conversation though. One that needed to be had with my family. I had hurt my ankle and used that as an excuse to run back home. I should have stayed and dealt with the family issues. I wasn't ready for that though. I was scared. See, my mom talks to God a lot. And when God tells her something, she immediately tells you. The thing is, everything she has told me was spot on. I had a feeling that she was going to read me, and I wasn't ready nor did I want to hear that at that time. I should have been woman enough to accept the correction that was coming and listen to what I needed.

While all of this was going on, my health was worse. I had gotten to the point where I was passing out. I passed out at the VA while walking back to get blood drawn. We thought it may have been because I hadn't eaten before the appointment. That wasn't it. They finally sent me to a cardiologist. My friend had suggested it could be my heart in that she had similar issues, and it was her heart. I was so nervous going to the appointment because I knew that heart disease ran rampant on my dad's and bio mom's sides of the family. The office did an echocardiogram and then ran several other tests. They set me up for what's called a tilt table test. What happens is you lie on a table. You are then tilted until you are upright. There is a pressure cuff on your arm, measuring your numbers. If your pressure spikes, or you pass out, you are determined to have some sort of tachycardia. I was ready to bite my nails having to wait til test day.

I was placed in another pain management. This time, Percocet. My body laughed at me. It was ridiculous. I just stopped going.

I was getting tired, and my body was over it. As time went on, I noticed that I was starting to have stomach issues. I was once again in and out of the hospital. I was to the point where I felt like I was dying. I could barely move. I didn't want to eat. It was so bad that my hair was matted. I couldn't figure out what was wrong with me.

My husband and I were at a point where we tolerated each other. What hurt the most was when I had to go to the hospital, he would just drop me off and leave me there. Several of the nurses knew my face, so when I came in by myself at times barely able to walk, they wondered where my husband was. I didn't tell them what was happening. They always ask if you feel safe at home. I felt safe but not safe. I was physically safe. I was not mentally and emotionally safe. At the time, I didn't know how to express that fully.

I had a new therapist as the one from the VA was getting married and moving. So she placed me in what is called community care. It allowed me to have a therapist a little closer to my house and who had a better schedule as she didn't have as many clients. Yes, all my therapists were women. And this one was another veteran. As I began seeing her, I realized that I needed to make the final change in my life. I needed a divorce. My therapist started talking to me about my medical symptoms. She then did a relation to how each issue was a respondent to stress, anger, grief, loss, and mental and emotional abuse. My eyes had finally opened.

That April, I went back home for my son's graduation celebration. My mom (bio) wanted to do something special for her oldest grandson graduating. It was a big deal for us. My oldest was getting ready to graduate. I couldn't believe it. The party was so much fun. I made my special baked beans. No matter what was happening or how I was feeling, cooking was my therapy. I had the most peace in the kitchen creating. Food and writing are my art. My self-expression. My son had the time of his life. Made enough money to pay his phone bill for the month and buy himself a video game. He was so glad to be almost done. His rough school life was almost over.

When you have a party with that side of the family, it's everything. We had a whole barbecue. Hamburgers, hotdogs, and we fixed a lot of sides. There was conversation and pictures. I would have these memories for a lifetime. I didn't tell anyone what was going on. My family was not too happy though that my husband was sending me places with the kids and he didn't attend either. They felt that with my medical issues, I shouldn't be driving by myself. My oldest didn't have his license yet. Yet, they didn't know how my husband felt toward them. That was an *if I told it, something not so good could happen.*

Year 14

I am very much a Daddy's girl. So at the end of June, I went home to visit my family and my bestie. I needed to make sure that I was making the right decision. I had for years been telling my father some of the issues I was having. The thing is, I didn't tell him everything. I knew my dad. If I had told him everything that had happened, I don't think my husband would have made it. Seriously. I also know my dad would have told me to leave a long time ago. You know you're going to be told the truth, but it's not what you want to hear, so you avoid certain conversations. It was time to tell the truth. Now my best friend knew more than my dad did. All of my friends did. But we all support each other until we are done with the situation. I was done.

I got home, and I spent time with my dad first. I let him know what was on my mind. I told him that I wanted a divorce. His words? Finally. It shocked me. Yet, as I talked to him more, I understood why. He told me that my mom had told him that my husband was still cheating on me. He also said that he wasn't happy that my husband had lied to him. When they first met, he promised my dad that if I got out of the Navy, he would work however many jobs he needed to make sure I, my son, and our soon-to-be son were taken care of. He didn't keep his word. I had also spoken to my dad about the cheating. I still had not told him about the STDs though. Again, I saved the man's life. My father 100% supported my decision, and let me know that he would be there for me through it all. He also prayed with me, because he knew the journey I was about to embark on was about to be hell.

I finally got to see my bestie of over 20 years. We had been cool since middle school. She was my second sister after my cousin. If I made a bad decision, she chewed me out and then comforted me. When she made a bad decision, I chewed her out and then asked if she wanted wine or ice cream. That was our dynamic. No wine for this situation though because I had stopped drinking a long time before, and she was very pregnant. We did go out to eat though so we could have privacy and no kids around. I was so glad to see her since I didn't get to the last two times. While we waited for our food, I laid on her the true purpose of the visit. She asked me what finally made me reach the point of wanting a divorce. I told her that I realized that even though I said I forgave my husband over and over again, I couldn't let go mentally and emotionally what he had done. I couldn't trust him anymore as much as I wanted to. My heart had left. My mind just needed to realize that the fantasy was over. My wish and my reality were the complete opposite. I began to tell her the things that I had only ever told my therapists, the deep things. There were no tears. Just despair from me. But after I told her, it was like someone lifted a weight off of me. I felt solid in my decision. Of course, she supported the decision and was glad I had finally reached the point of no return, ergo she felt it took way too long to get to that point. We are blatantly honest with each other, even when it hurts because we know that's what the other wants to hear. We don't sugarcoat anything between us. I was so thankful for her loving me through my stupid moments, days, and years.

I went home, with my mind reeling. In my head, there were so many different scenarios. I knew that my husband owned a gun and I didn't know if he would try to use it or not. I knew I needed to tell him as calmly as possible. I also wanted the kids to be safe in the situation. I didn't want them hurt or used. I knew they didn't know what was going on. I never told them what was happening between myself and their father. So it was a long 8-hour ride home.

We arrived at the house, and I pulled into the garage. My heart was pounding like crazy. I was so nervous. My mouth was dry like I had been eating flour. I opened the door, looked right at my husband, and stated, "I want a divorce." He looked at my oldest as I kept walking to our room. I knew he was shocked, but I didn't care. I sat down on the bed and he and the kids got the luggage and other things out of the car. He then came into the room, shut the door, and began asking me what was going on. I told him everything that was on my mind. Everything that I was feeling. Every thought that I had pushed to the back of my mind came pouring out. I was done with him. I was over trying to constantly forgive him for cheating. I had honestly not let go of the situation with my son that I had to take off of the ventilator and bury. I wasn't over the STDs. I didn't trust him. I was done with the lack of his heart. I was the person who always gave, would randomly buy things that made me think of him and give them to him. I had memorized his favorite meal at every restaurant and fast food place we went to. He didn't take me on dates anymore. I had to beg for gifts for Christmas and my birthday. He never appreciated anything I did for him. I purchased clothes and all. I invested in his every dream, yet was always hearing I wasn't helping the way he wanted or needed. I was tired. My mind and body were tired. I wasn't in love with him anymore. He sat there looking crazy like he and I had never had these conversations before. For years, I had been asking him to change as I was changing how I needed to and he asked me to. I was done doing all the work. I wanted to be a woman and be treated like a woman, instead of having to be the man in the relationship.

My oldest knocked on the door, wanting to come in. I let him into the room. He started asking why I wanted a divorce. I told him his dad could explain it to him. He didn't tell him the whole story at that point, just that I was still angry over some things from the past. That explanation didn't even fully convey everything I had said. Then my husband tried to bring up what the Bible said about divorce. What? Don't do that sir. It's not the road you want to take. He started ranting, and I tuned out. Suddenly, it seemed like it had turned into the Spanish Inquisition. He was asking a whole bunch of why questions. I don't even remember half of them. My son had left and gone to his room. I didn't realize my middle and youngest were listening until I looked at the door. I just walked to them, hugged them, and told them I was sorry. They started to cry. I held them in my arms. Over the next few days, my husband would sit down and talk to the kids. He finally told the kids what he had done which had pushed me to the point of where I was. My youngest didn't understand, but my middle and oldest did. They kept asking me why I couldn't forgive one last time. I couldn't do it. I didn't have the energy for it anymore.

Thus began a litany of craziness. Every day I was asked questions. At one point, he said he wanted to do marriage counseling. I had been asking for that for years. I also let him know that marriage counseling did no good if he didn't put in the work to get counseling himself. He wouldn't do it. I still agreed to the marriage counseling even though my heart and mind were already decided. My counselor set the date for the next day. We sat in front of the computer together. She asked my husband several questions. She also asked him why he wanted to do marriage counseling now instead of all the other times I asked him to do it. He said he didn't realize the marriage was so bad until now. She then asked him to ask me what I wanted and how I felt. I told him that at that point it was too late. I was ready to put my energy into getting the kids through the separation and divorce. I guess he started speaking to her on his own because she let me know that he said if I divorced him, he wasn't going to see the kids anymore. He didn't want to be reminded I divorced him. Then he told her that he wasn't going to help financially. I guess at some point he went back and told her he had changed his mind.

My husband started to act strange. He would no longer eat the food I cooked. He had stopped eating altogether. It was so bad I called an ambulance to come check him out. I told 911 no police. They still sent a unit, and they arrived before the ambulance did. I had to go into protection mode because I didn't want anything to happen considering the gun was in the house. This man thought I had called the police on him. It was the dumbest thing ever. Just because I wanted a divorce didn't mean I wanted something bad to happen to him. He refused to be checked, so I left it alone.

I told my bio mom that I wanted a divorce. That whole conversation was a mess. She tried to tell me God didn't say for me to leave my marriage, that I was wrong, that I should keep trying. Forget what the whole situation had done to me in every facet. I hung up on her. She then texted me telling me I should stop listening to the devil. Really? I wanted so badly to say certain things to her about her divorce from my dad, but I left it alone. I had to call my dad right after so I could get some encouragement because I was on a different level of anger. I felt old parts of me trying to come back, and it wasn't necessary with the situation at hand. My dad helped me calm down. He was livid about what my mom had said to me. He couldn't believe it.

My husband decided he wanted to randomly be sweet. He went to Walmart saying that he needed to pick something up. He returned with roses and a card. Sir!! You can't buy me back. He stood there, so I opened and read the card. I told him thank you. He asked for a hug. I stiffly hugged him. He left again, and I called my best friend. I had to get that thing off my chest. While on the phone with her, I threw the card in the trash. I don't even remember what he wrote in it. I told her what happened. She told me I should get rid of the flowers too. I didn't want to, but I also agreed it would send the wrong message, and that's not wanted to convey. After we got off the phone, I had to go into the bathroom. Apparently at some point my husband had returned and was quite angry. He went into my trash can on my side of the room and pulled the card out. He claimed he had to throw something away and that was why he was in my trash. The thing is, he had a whole trash can on his side of the room. He asked me why I threw it away. I told him the gesture was late and lacked any meaning. You've lost me, and now you want to try to win me back. Yet the entire fourteen years of marriage I had told him how to keep me. Too little, too late. He complained about the money wasted. I said nothing.

One day, things with my husband boiled over. He had started with the questions once again. I was exasperated with feeling like I was being interrogated. I don't remember what he asked, but I finally went off. I told him all his decisions were trash. I said a lot more, but I don't even remember what. Suddenly, he pulled out his gun and put it to his head. I yelled at my oldest to take my keys and go to my car with his brothers. My son looked in the room and saw how my husband was sitting. I also told my son to call either his grandfather or grandmother. I wanted to make sure my children were safe. I told my son if he heard a shot go off to leave. I knew he couldn't drive, but if he could just get down the street he and his brother would be safe. I'm sure he was probably really scared, but I couldn't focus on that at the moment. I slowly sat back down on the bed once I heard the door to the garage close. I looked my husband right in his eyes, and calmly but forcefully said "I bind and rebuke that spirit right now in the name of Jesus." It was almost like the trance broke, and he put the gun down. He then burst into tears and begged me not to divorce him. He said it made him feel like he was a failure. I didn't say anything.

I texted my bio mom, my dad, and my bestie to let them know what had happened. My bio mom was telling me that I had pushed my husband to want to hurt himself. I didn't even message her back. My dad called me and made sure me and the kids were ok. He told me I should have called the police and let them handle it. I told my dad at that point that I just wanted the man to leave. I felt he was a danger to myself and the kids. While

I was talking to my dad, he was outside on his phone. But at the same time, he was listening to my conversation. I never did that to him when he was making whatever phone calls he needed to. They were not my business anymore at that point. I was hoping he was making arrangements to go wherever he needed to. I was going to let the separation stall out for a few more months so he could get money saved so he didn't have to be homeless. My mind was completely changed at that point.

I had started going to church after that. He decided he was going to go too. Once again, too little too late. He tried to make it seem like we just needed some spiritual guidance and that God was completely against us getting a divorce. He felt like I was praying against us instead of for us. I was praying that I would be set free. The next day, he had an interview in another city to be a boy's counselor. That fell through because they said he was too small. So his mom told him he could come stay with her until he got on his feet. She had texted me telling me it would be hard to raise three sons on my own. I told her I would be just fine. I had Jesus, friends, and family.

I had pulled down and printed off a separation agreement. That was we had a plan in place for everything. He would not sign it. He began packing his things to leave. He claimed he spoke to the police, and that they told him to leave because I was causing him mental damage. The day he put the gun to his head was my fault. He said he was keeping them from arresting me by leaving. I believed nothing he said since I had already talked to a lawyer the day after he had put the gun to his head. So I knew it was nothing but drama. He thought I would beg him to stay. I sat right there as he packed. He began getting rid of all the bears, cards, and everything else I bought him. He gave some of them to the kids. My babies were crying as he finished putting his belongings in his truck. He also put the cat in the truck since he bought him. I asked him repeatedly to leave Kevin with us because the kids loved him and we had no issues taking care of him. That man wasn't even trying to hear that. I told the kids we would just have to buy another pet. I told my husband to let me know when he made it to his destination. He said goodbye, and pulled off. Everyone went back to their rooms. About 30 minutes later, I received a call from him saying that the cat had escaped when he went to fix something in his SUV. I found that hard to believe because that's not how the cat was at all. I said ok, and told the kids what had happened. Tears were flowing again.

About an hour later, the doorbell rang. A guy had come by saying he had found a cat in the parking lot. He had a chip scanner and it showed that Kevin lived at our house. He asked if we wanted him or should he take him to the shelter. I immediately jumped in the car to follow the guy so I could get Kevin back. God had made a way for Kevin to come home. The kids were so excited. I had to call my dad to borrow some money so I could get food, bowls, litter, and a litter box. My husband had taken everything with him. I was so glad that my children were going to have some peace.

A few days later, I had my tilt table test. I was ready for answers. My blood pressure had rocketed so high it wasn't funny. The doctor couldn't say definitively, but she believed I had something called POTS. POTS (Postural Orthostatic Tachycardia Syndrome) is a syndrome usually triggered when a person stands up after lying down. It most commonly affects women between the ages of 15 and 50. Symptoms include lightheadedness, fainting, and rapid heartbeat, which are relieved by lying down again. I was for a long life of yet another change. One thing I did do though once my husband left is come off a lot of my medications. I was taking a total of 14 different medications. I cut that in half. My goal was to wean myself off until I was taking on the necessary ones. This included the mental health meds.

As time went by, it seemed as if a fog was lifting from my brain. Things seemed to just feel lighter. The only problem I was having was sleeping at night. It felt like someone was laying on top of me when I tried to sleep at night. I didn't sleep for 8 days straight. Literally. I called and told my dad what was happening. He told me that I was fighting the spiritual tie I had to my husband and the demonic spirits were trying to attack me in my sleep. A sister hurried up and started fasting and praying. I asked the ladies from my church to help me pray also. I wanted to be free. This was one heck of a battle. But I finally won. On day nine, I slept for the longest I had slept in a long time. It was peaceful. It was rejuvenating. It was another sign that I had made the right decision.

I was attempting to start my middle and youngest homeschooling again. They were struggling. My middle son was so used to his dad helping him with his schoolwork. Both boys seemed to be depressed. I didn't want to push them too hard. At the same time, we needed to create a new and better schedule. My oldest had wanted to get a job and found one at Walmart around Thanksgiving. I was so proud of him for pushing his way to his first job. He had graduated back in May, the day before my birthday. It was the perfect birthday present for me.

My husband came by to visit the kids off and on. He didn't want to come because he didn't want to see me. The first time he came to visit was so awkward. It felt weird even attempting to hug him. The atmosphere felt all wrong. He left the same day. A few weeks later, he showed up but I didn't know he was there. The kids said they tried to wake me up and tell me he was coming. All I remember is they tried to wake me up and told them to leave me alone. He was not happy about how I felt about it. After what happened with the gun issue, I needed to know when he was coming so I could prepare myself. He said he wanted to be there for my oldest first day at work. I understood wanting to be a part of that special day. Just give me the courtesy of letting me know. Once again, he left the same day. The next time he came was Christmas. He had asked me what I wanted to cook and he would pay for it. Granted, he knew I wasn't going to beg him for anything. I had asked for gas money a few times, and he told me he didn't have it when I knew he did. He had been working at Walmart for a few months. He got the job right after he returned to Virginia. It was what it was though. The kids had asked for Nerf guns. I said no. He purchased them anyway. I was livid. We had a text argument when he left because I wasn't going to argue in front of the kids. They had been through enough.

Income tax time was getting ready to come around. The discussion was to file jointly since even though we were separated, he had been there for over 6 months before he left. I would send him a copy of my driver's license, and we would split the money in half. That was the plan. He decided at the last minute he wanted to change the plan after I had already sent him my driver's license and the kids' information. I was heated. Something fishy was going on. I just didn't know what.

My car ended up messed up, so I had to purchase a new one. I managed to get it with no money down since I had purchased my last car from that dealership. I would have traded in the other car, but because my name and my husband's name were on it, I couldn't do anything. I even wanted to sell the car since it was just taking up room in the garage. My kids had not seen their father since Christmas. It was breaking their hearts. He even stopped texting them as much. I decided to have the middle and youngest begin therapy to help them navigate their feelings. I knew the time for the divorce was coming up, and I wanted to be able to face it head-on. I also needed my children to be able to come to me with what they were feeling.

My birthday came around, and we did something different that year. I was always doing it for everyone for their birthday. But my husband had not taught my sons how to buy a gift from their hearts. So I told my oldest to pick a cake and card from his heart for my birthday. He had started working at Food Lion, so I asked his manager to help him since she was a mom. He brought home the cutest cake and semi-sweetest card. He did it for me and picked a card that talked trash. I still loved it. The cake was divided between everyone as we always do. The next day, we went to Golden Corral. It was so much fun. It was our first time going out since everything happened. It felt good to spend so much time with my sons.

Year 15 and the Ending

Year 15 came around. My husband texted me Happy Anniversary. I had nothing to say to him. I didn't have anything to say to him. He told the kids the reason why he hadn't come to see them was because his mom's boyfriend had died, and he was hurting. I'm not even going to go into the details of the relationship between the two of them. I stopped talking to him after he constantly tried to remind me of the past instead of just concentrating on the kids. Then he made the promise he would see them every week. He lied. I couldn't depend on him, so for extra money, I donated blood. It covered what I needed for gas in between paychecks. Yes, I had filed for child support. He was sent papers to go to court. I was kind enough to remind him of the court dates and when they were because I had received the same notices. I realized that he wanted to avoid taking care of his children. When there was a need for extra food, he would send the least amount and the cheapest items.

My middle son ended up needing shoes because somehow his feet grew quickly in the three months since I had last purchased his shoes. I didn't have the extra funds at the time, as I had to make sure there was enough money to take my oldest to work for a couple of days until he was paid. It felt like pulling teeth. That was all my middle son wanted from his father for his birthday. That and him coming to see him. He only did one. He purchased the shoes. They were the wrong size, so I had to exchange them. My son was still hurt because he felt his father didn't love him anymore. He didn't even call him on his birthday. I had to call my dad and have him talk to my son. It was the last time my son cried over his father. It hurt the most because it was his 13th birthday. My son had officially become a teenager. He hit one of the biggest milestones of his life.

A few weeks later, my husband let me know he wanted to come by. I told him I was ok with it. My youngest was still very attached to his father, even though therapy was helping him deal with the emotions that came with having to watch his father leave. My oldest had disassociated with everything when it came to him. I wanted him to go to therapy, but with him being an adult, I had to find an alternative. My dad would talk to him as often as possible so he didn't become depressed. I still made a point to talk to each son daily just to see what was on their minds and how they were feeling.

My husband showed up, and we had a decent conversation. He and I went to the DMV, and he signed the car over to me. I was grateful that he did that. While we were at the DMV, we talked about what was going on in his life. He claimed he was seeing a counselor, and he and the counselor were trying to figure out why he was continually trying to create a family. He said that he wanted to have another child. I looked at him like he was crazy. He was on child support for 2 kids and wasn't helping take care of our two. Why would you want to bring another life into the turmoil that is already in your life? I couldn't even deal. We went back to the house, then he went to get himself something to eat and buy the kids some gifts. I asked him if he could treat them but he said he didn't have the money. The only problem I had with that was he had said he just got paid, and I knew how much he was getting paid an hour. I felt there were lies somewhere in there, but I let it go. I wasn't about to give the third degree. His money was going somewhere, and it wasn't to take care of his children. He came back, watched the kids open their presents, put things together, made sure the toys had batteries, and an hour later was gone. He had to turn back around because I called him about how hard the youngest one was crying. He hugged the kids again, talked to them, and left again. I had a feeling that was the last time my children were going to see him.

My husband had started sending weird text messages. He claimed they were his friend's wife, but they didn't make any sense. The woman was saying that her daughter wasn't going to be a narcissist and would know if she was with a narcissist. I say woman because of the way the conversation was going. But she made it sound like it was my husband speaking. When I asked him about it, he said it wasn't him and that he would leave his phone unlocked because he would use it at work and there was no need to lock it. I knew better than that. I believed he had a girlfriend and possibly a baby on the way. The text messages just did too much. The final nail in the coffin for me was a picture he sent to my son's phone. It was of a PS5 on a bed. The other problem I had with that is he said he was homeless and sleeping in his truck. So why would you buy a game system if you have nowhere to plug it up? The lies were piling up, and he was trying to draw my children into them. All the times he claimed he was at his friend's house, I believe he was with whoever he was with house. I don't play about my children. Hurt me. But leave them my babies alone.

The next month, in August, I filed for divorce. I was ready to be free. My one-year sentence was up. I borrowed the money to pay the fees. I wasn't going to wait any longer. Myself and another woman received the same court date. We were so excited!! Back in June, I started working on my Bachelor's degree in Psychology with a concentration in mental health counseling. I was making some dreams come true. On top of that, God had laid on my heart to start searching for a new place for myself and my children. I couldn't stay in North Carolina anymore. There was nothing there for us. I had found a home that I fell in love with. Everyone would have their own room. The yard was huge. The kids would have more than enough room to play and have a garden. Kevin could live his best life. One day, I called my dad so he could do a virtual walk-through of the house with me since he had purchased a house before and knew what to look for if there were any issues. As we were talking and looking at the pictures, my dad said something random. He said the house was going to cost $189,000. Well, that was crazy because the house I was looking at was $220,00. I knew the Holy Spirit was speaking through him, and I needed to trust God. Close to my court date, I began doing more research into the house. The realtor tried to get the seller to accept the VA loan, but he wouldn't budge. So the realtor sent me a list of houses that were for sale in the area I was looking at. Lo and behold, there was a beautiful 5 bedroom 2 bathroom home for the same price my dad told me. I knew this was my and my children's home. I asked the realtor to put in the offer. It was accepted. We were going to be moving!!

Court day, September 22, finally came around. Before I arrived at the courthouse, my First Lady at church called to pray with me. Then my bio mom called to pray with me. My adopted aunt from my oldest son's job called to give me a pep talk. When I posted on Facebook I was getting ready to walk in, the love poured in. My heart was beating like crazy. At first, I had a problem finding the correct courtroom. When I finally found it, I had to fill out the paperwork that would be the final decree. It looked strange compared to my first one, but I didn't care. I had requested child support in the paperwork I filed with the court, but because I had already started the process with the Child Support office, I had to take it up with them. I was only in the courtroom for about 15 minutes. A lot of people didn't show up. I was called up and swore that the information I gave was true. They looked to see if my husband was there (he never showed up even though he was notified), and just like that, I was free. I paid the extra to make sure my name was changed back to my maiden name. It was finished. God had shown up and showed out again. And He was just getting started.

I got in the car and cried. It felt so releasing. Yes, I grieved the fact that things didn't work. I grieved the hurt and pain. I grieved what my children had been through. I grieved the lies and choices. I let it all go. From that day forward, I refused to allow myself to ever be put through that again. Right after I went straight to the Social Security office. I was changing all my information back. When I finished there, I drove to the VA office to change my Veteran's ID. I couldn't change that until my social security card came back, and I had my new license. I was about to be on that too. I set up that appointment and eagerly awaited the next week.

The same week I filed for my divorce, my younger sons and I were in a car accident. I was taking them to the dentist. I went to make a right-hand turn, and a guy slammed into the back of me. Blessedly there were witnesses right across the street who saw everything. I was grateful for them. The accident messed up my head, my neck, and my back. So the car I had just started paying on earlier that year was done for. Fortunately, the man's insurance paid for the rental. I had to go get yet another car.

So I had to clear some things before my loan could be written for my house. New license, insurance pays off the car, and the escrow payment. I paid the escrow as soon as I got paid. So that meant I had more time. I was trying to get out of the house by the end of October, as that was when our lease was up. God made a way for us to get a new car within days. A few days later, I was able to get my new license, and then a new Veterans ID. I began to stalk the car company. The insurance had paid off a large portion of the car, and the gap insurance was supposed to cover the rest. It was an option I started not to take when I purchased the car, but I was thankful I listened to the Holy Spirit and took it. Finally, the car was fully paid for and off my credit. It was official. The notary from the loan company came by, and I signed the paperwork for my new home. My mind couldn't wrap around it.

We had already begun packing up the house. I had the kids start in August, doing a little at a time. Now we were in crunch time. My husband told my youngest son he was going to stop by for his birthday. No discussion with me. No sir. Not going to happen. I had asked him more than once to speak to me if he wanted to come see the kids. I knew he still owned his gun. So he was mad. He didn't even do anything for my oldest birthday, no more than to tell him Happy Birthday. He went out with his friends and had an incredible time, so I wasn't going to fuss about what my ex-husband didn't do. My ex-husband did send something for my middle and youngest. They were grateful, but I could tell that it didn't mean as much to them.

Everything was finally packed. I told the kids we could take what fit in the car. We still had to put the cat in. We had a long drive ahead of us. We had our last meal in North Carolina, heading to IHOP for breakfast. The kids were so excited. I was ecstatic. We were about to begin a new life.

We have been here for 3 months now. The house is even more beautiful in person. We've even had the chance to meet and talk to the former owners. My younger sons hadn't heard from their father since October. They decided they didn't want to speak to him anymore. I told them I would support whatever decision they made. My oldest hasn't heard from him since December. God removed him completely. I don't even want child support anymore. I just pray that he doesn't damage another child or woman. I pray that he receives the help and healing that he needs. He's in God's hands. I am searching for a church home here. I'm still homeschooling my sons, and they are so happy and have so much peace. I have peace. I love it here.

Epilogue

Here's what I learned from this whole experience. You can't give your love to just anyone. Some people don't know how to appreciate who you are. It's ok to love people from a distance. Don't accept mediocrity. Don't think you can fix a broken person. Sometimes you're meant to only be in their lives long enough to help them see their brokenness. More than like you're not meant to be there permanently. How you define love and how someone else defines love are two different definitions.

To my Christian ladies, don't allow anyone to use the Bible to beat you into staying in a relationship that is abusive, downgrading, and the man constantly cheats on you. If he wanted to change he would. Sometimes God isn't trying to fix the situation, He's trying to fix you. If you keep hearing "leave", and it's over and over from different people, some who know you and some who don't, maybe take the time to pay attention. God does not want His daughters hurt. Your husband should love you as much as he loves himself. If he loves you less than himself, he either doesn't love himself or thinks he's better. Don't let yourself be trampled over. Your children see that. Don't let them see their mother being treated badly. Your daughter will think it's ok to be treated that way, and your sons will think it's ok to act that way.

Mental illness is a heavy load. All it takes is the right trauma to crack open the coconut. If you see signs of mental illness, get help. It's ok to go to therapy or counseling. It's ok to get help. Stigmas don't matter. What matters is your mental, emotional, spiritual, and physical health. Being unhealthy can kill you. An unhealthy mind, unhealthy emotions, and an unhealthy spirit manifest physically. It may be why your blood pressure is so high. Why you have constant headaches. You can't sleep at night because your mind is constantly in shambles. Heal before it's too late.

It's ok to take responsibility for bad decisions. But don't let anyone beat you over the head the fact that you made bad decisions. You heal and move on. Don't wallow in that place. People can only do to you what you allow them to.

Forgiveness is your power, not theirs. Forgiveness allows you to release whoever hurt you back into the wild. Understand the grudge you hold against them, they're not even thinking about it. That person has probably moved on in life, and you're still stuck in that same place. Hurt people hurt people. You don't have to keep suffering that hurt. You deserve your freedom. So take it back. That doesn't mean you always need it face-to-face. If the chance comes, then safely forgive that person to his or her face. If the chance never comes, in your heart and mind say, "I forgive you and I release you and myself." Then truly let it go.

I'm including a list of affirmations that I created last year. I pray that they help you like they have me.

Thank you for reading my book. Please share with as many others as you can.

Always and Forever

Lady Candi Usher

Daily Affirmations

1. I am loved and worthy of love
2. I am strong.   3. I am a conquer
4. I am a winner   5. I am beautiful/handsome
6. I will smile through it all. 7. I am a Queen/King
8. I love others as much as I love myself, and I love me some me.
9. I will keep my head up through the storms
10. Others don't define me
11. I can't be stopped. The only one in my way is me.
12. I am fierce, mighty, a fighter until the end
13. I will love, I will forgive, I will move on
14. I was created for a purpose, and I will live up to that purpose when I find it
15. I deserve someone who will walk in purpose with me
16. I will not stand for abuse nor will I allow myself to be misused and abused.

Daily Affirmations